WINNING *the* WITNESSES

Daniel Rodriguez

Edited by David W. Daniels

CHICK
PUBLICATIONS
Ontario, Calif 91761

For a complete list of distributors near you,
call (909) 987-0771, or visit
www.chick.com

Copyright ©2007 by Daniel Rodriguez

Published by:
CHICK PUBLICATIONS
PO Box 3500, Ontario, Calif. 91761-1019 USA
Tel: (909) 987-0771
Fax: (909) 941-8128
Web: www.chick.com
Email: postmaster@chick.com

Printed in the United States of America

First Printing

ISBN: 978-07589-0674-8

Scripture quotations: King James Version and *The New
World Translation* (Watchtower Bible and Tract Society)

The organization of the Watchtower Bible and Tract Society is referred to in this book as the "Watchtower" or "Watchtower Society." The magazine published by the Watchtower Society is referred to as *"Watchtower"* or *"The Watchtower."*

PART ONE
BASICS OF WATCHTOWER SOCIETY THEOLOGY

1 The Watchtower Society: The Source of Interpretation and Control 13

- Why Jehovah's Witnesses Depend upon the Watchtower Society 16

- How The Watchtower Society Controls the Jehovah's Witness 19

2 The Watchtower's Purpose and Eternal Value 23

- How The Watchtower Society Trains Jehovah's Witnesses 26

- Their Primary Book for Study 27

- Challenging and Undermining The Watchtower Society's Message 30

- Beliefs Based Solely on the Bible? 31
- Getting the Witness to Question the Need for The Watchtower Society 32

- Is The Watchtower Inspired of God? 34

- False Watchtower Prophecies 36

PART TWO
CREATING AN EFFECTIVE WITNESSING STRATEGY

3 Key Elements to an Effective Witness 43

- Implementing Your Witnessing Strategy . 44

4 Did Jesus Die on a Cross? 51

- Indecison in *The Watchtower* 53
- How Does the Bible Say Jesus Died? 57
- Implementing Your Witnessing Strategy . 59
- The Decision for Truth 62

5 Who Resurrected Jesus? 65

- Jehovah God Resurrected Jesus 66
- Jesus' Role in His Own Resurrection 67
- The Holy Spirit's Role in
  Jesus' Resurrection 69

PART THREE
WHAT HAPPENS AFTER THEY ARE SAVED?

6 Cost of Leaving The Watchtower Society . . 75

- The Trauma of Shattered Faith 76
- The Loss of Family and Security 78
- Holding on to What Was 81
- Disciple With Patience 82

7 Showing the Plan of Salvation 85

- Your Witnessing Strategy 87
- Jehovah's Witness Tactics 88
- Questions for the Witness 89

8 The Journey to Grace 99

- Discipling Tips 100
- Share Your Testimony 100
- Engage in Activities 101
- The Issue of Trust 102
- The Decision for Christ 103
- God Loves to Give 105

I heartily endorse the method, content and style of "Winning The Witnesses." Daniel has studied the issue carefully and has "hands on" experience as well.

> Don Nelson
> Former Jehovah's Witness missionary
> and Circuit Overseer in Brazil and the U.S.

My 12-year-old daughter used Daniel's strategies to witness to a Jehovah's Witness friend at school. Within a few weeks, the witnessing spread to the rest of the family. My daughter led her friend to the Lord. In time, the rest of the family came to accept Christ, including an uncle and his family. They had been in the Watchtower for 27 years. Today, they are serving the Lord.

Our neighbor had been studying with the Witnesses for about a year and was set to be baptized in the organization. Daniel Rodriguez showed us how to witness to her. She was thoroughly indoctrinated and put up quite a fight, but within two days, she admitted the Watchtower was not of God and gave her heart to Christ.

A Jehovah's Witness neighbor came to witness to me. Using the strategies Daniel Rodriguez taught me, my neighbor gave his heart to Christ. He could not resist the wisdom in the witnessing strategy and could no longer be a Jehovah's Witnesses. To this day, he is serving the Lord.

8

Preface

Imagine that you had a fresh, new approach, a "key" that would unlock the hearts and minds of the Jehovah's Witnesses. Imagine that, once unlocked, you could effectively present the good news of Jesus Christ.

To do this, you must understand how the Witnesses arrive at their beliefs. Otherwise, your discussion will become a scripture shouting match, yielding little or no results.

Christians with good intentions usually hit an unseen barrier — a communication gap that stands between them and the Jehovah's Witnesses. To cross this gap, the Christian must recognize that the Witness understands and interprets the Bible only through the authority of the Watchtower Bible and Tract Society. He is not free to have a personal or private interpretation. Before any effective witnessing can be done, the Christian must first be prepared to call into question this Watchtower authority.

Part one of this book will describe the basics of the Watchtower theology so you can understand where the problem of communication exists between the Christian and the Jehovah's Witnesses.

Part two will teach you effective witnessing strategies, showing you how to raise doubt in the mind of the Jehovah's

Witness about the authority of *The Watchtower.* The individual Witness is not where the communication problem lies; the problem is the authority to which the individual Witness has submitted himself.

As long as the Jehovah's Witness reads the Bible through the colored glasses of the Watchtower, no arguments or proof texts will ever persuade him. He will continue to defend what he holds to be truth as revealed by the Jehovah's Witness organization. But if his confidence in the authority of the Watchtower can be destroyed, you will have a candidate ready to listen to the pure gospel of Jesus Christ.

Keep in mind that, as the Witnesses go door to door, their mission is to teach the public Jehovah's truths. The Christian feels that he has to fulfill the Great Commission and go into combat to persuade the Jehovah's Witness that he is wrong. This strategy seldom works. *We must use wisdom in witnessing* to Jehovah's Witnesses. The strategies outlined in this book have been proven by winning many Jehovah's Witnesses to Christ.

It is my prayer that the Lord will use His people to lead many out of the Watchtower Society into the Kingdom of His dear Son.

Part One
Basics of Watchtower Society Theology

CHAPTER 1

The Watchtower Society: The Source of Interpretation and Control

JW: Good morning.

Christian: Good morning.

JW: We are ministers who are calling upon the neighborhood this morning. I'm sure that you'll agree the condition of this world has been getting worse and there seems to be no real end in sight.

Christian: Uh-huh. Are you two Jehovah's Witnesses?

JW: Why yes....we are.

Christian: I appreciate you stopping by but my pastor tells me that you people simply do not read the Bible.

JW: Excuse me. Your pastor is mistaken. We do read the Bible.

Christian: Well, you read another kind of Bible.

JW: Well, that's not what we're interested in discussing today. We are here to announce hope for this present system of things. As you know, we live in probably the most violent time known to mankind and God...

Christian: Yes, that may be true, but I am told that Jehovah's Witnesses are a cult. Look. What about the hope of heaven for all who accept Jesus as Lord? Shouldn't that be the true message of the gospel?

JW: Uh, excuse me but we are not a cult and we do not want to go to heaven. Our hope is to remain on paradise earth.

Christian: What? What do you mean you don't want to go to heaven? Jesus said, "I am the way, the truth and the life." He also said that He went to prepare a place for us and where He is we can be there too.

JW: Well, it's apparent that you have other things in mind besides thinking of what God's will is for you. Thank you for your time.

Christian: Wait! I have one more question on...

JW: Sir, we did not come here to debate. It's obvious that you are not open to the truth. Thank you for your time.

This scenario has been played out countless times in homes around the world. Christians think that if they present enough Biblical proof texts and "outgun" the Jehovah's Witnesses, this will somehow persuade them that they are wrong and make them see the true message of the gospel of Jesus Christ.

The end result is both parties arguing — each attempting to persuade the other that he is wrong. As the Witness leaves, the Christian may feel triumphant, believing he made his case.

Unknown to the Christian, the Witnesses are thoroughly trained in how to respond to those who oppose their message. I can assure you that nothing was accomplished.

The Witnesses have a very powerful tool at their disposal and they are masters of their craft. Their tool is the publications of The Watchtower Society. For those not grounded in the Word, The Watchtower Society is a very persuasive and powerful force to be reckoned with.

At this writing, 6,741,444 people worldwide have accepted the message of The Watchtower Society as their truth.

Of this impressive figure, about 50% were Catholics and about 20% were from various Protestant denominations. This does not include those Witnesses who were raised in this religion throughout its 128-year history.

Why Jehovah's Witnesses Depend Upon The Watchtower Society

How would you react to a pagan's interpretation of the Bible? Would you allow yourself to be taught by a pagan and submit to his leadership and theology as your authority? The answer is "No!"

You need to understand that the Jehovah's Witnesses are taught that every religion outside of the Watchtower Society is pagan in origin. They believe that in 1919 Jehovah God founded the Watchtower Society alone to possess the truths that they had been proclaiming since July, 1879.

You would never accept a pagan's interpretation of the Bible as the truth. Well, guess what? The Jehovah's Witnesses have as much respect for you and your theology as you do for paganism. The Witnesses are taught that everything you hold to be true as a Christian, including the Trinity and the person of the Holy Spirit, has its roots in paganism.

What message are they taking door to door?

Believe it or not, they are taking The Watchtower's interpretation of the Bible in their attempt to crush paganism. Each Witness carries this message as an emissary of the Watchtower Society — irritating many a Christian. But the Christian has made a big mistake: he believes that the Jehovah's Witnesses are the "problem." They are not. The *real* enemies are the doctrines The Watchtower Society teaches, not the Witnesses themselves.

Without the Watchtower Society's interpretation of the

Bible, the Witnesses will not be able to progress spiritually. Their magazine states:

> Unless we are in touch with this channel of communication that God is using [The Watchtower Society's leadership], we will not progress along the road to life, no matter how much Bible reading we do.[1]

The Watchtower Society teaches that one needs to be in touch with God's "human channel" before the Bible can be accurately understood.

> God caused the Bible to be written in such a way that one needs to be in touch with His human channel before one can fully and accurately understand it.[2]

The Watchtower Society also teaches that people need "Jehovah's visible organization" to understand the Bible:

> Thus the Bible is an organizational book and belongs to the Christian congregation as an organization, not to individuals, regardless of how sincerely they may believe they can interpret the Bible. *For this reason the Bible cannot be properly understood without Jehovah's visible organization in mind.*[3]

From these statements it is evident why the Jehovah's

---

1) *The Watchtower*, Dec. 1, 1981, p. 27.
2) The Watchtower, Feb. 15, 1981, p. 17.
3) The Watchtower, Oct. 1, 1967, p. 587.

Witnesses rely solely on the Watchtower Society's interpretation of scripture. It is also evident that the message they bring to your doorstep is not *their* message; it is The Watchtower Society's. This is the authority to which the Jehovah's Witnesses have submitted themselves.

The Watchtower Society's interpretation of the Bible cannot be penetrated with what they believe to be your "pagan arguments." This is why they reject your arguments when you use scripture in an attempt to witness to them: you are a "pagan" and are not in touch with "Jehovah's visible organization," according to what they are taught to believe.

Summary

- Jehovah's Witnesses believe your interpretation of the scriptures is pagan in origin.

- Because they have submitted themselves to Watchtower authority, they believe that Jehovah God gave only the Watchtower Society His truths.

- The message the Jehovah's Witnesses take door to door is The Watchtower's interpretation of the Bible. They believe this will help crush paganism.

- The real enemy is what The Watchtower Society says — not the Witnesses themselves.

- Your arguments from scripture do not work because the Witnesses believe your interpretation of the Bible comes from pagan sources.

- The Watchtower Society teaches that the Bible

"cannot be properly understood without Jehovah's visible organization [including *The Watchtower* magazine] in mind."

- The message of the Jehovah's Witness is not "Bible truth" he learned by himself; it is "Bible truth" the Watchtower Society *gave* him.

How The Watchtower Society Controls the Jehovah's Witness

To understand Jehovah's Witnesses *you* need to understand how they think. Only then will you understand why they use *The Watchtower* in their witnessing strategy.

The Witnesses believe that your faith is influenced by paganism and must come under the control of the Watchtower Society's authority and interpretation of scripture. Remember this: over half of the Witnesses who will knock on your door were at one time former Catholics, and about 20% were Protestants. They *already know* what you believe.

The following points will illustrate that not only the source of the Witnesses message, but his own reasoning and thinking, comes *only* from what is taught by the Watchtower Society. The Witness is merely mimicking what the Society wants him to be — a walking *Watchtower* magazine.

POINT 1: The Watchtower Society uses *The Watchtower* to teach Jehovah's "Bible truths," but they also use these publications to keep their followers in lock-step obedience.

Theocratic ones [Jehovah's Witnesses] will

appreciate the Lord's visible organization and not be *so foolish as to pit against Jehovah's channel their own human reasoning and sentiment and personal feelings.*[4]

He [the Jehovah's Witness] does *not advocate or insist on personal opinions or harbor private ideas when it comes to Bible understanding.* Rather, he has complete confidence in the truth as it is revealed by Jehovah God through his son, Jesus Christ, and "the faithful and discreet slave" [Watchtower leadership].[5]

POINT 2: The Jehovah's Witnesses are forbidden to think outside of the message of *The Watchtower. The Watchtower* stresses the urgency of being guided by the organization. Without it they are lost.

Avoid Independent Thinking. How is such independent thinking manifested? A common way is by questioning the counsel that is provided by God's visible organization.[6]

Fight against Independent Thinking. Such thinking is evidence of pride. If we get to thinking that we know better than the organization, we should ask ourselves: "Where did we learn Bible truth in the first place? Would

---

4) *The Watchtower*, Feb. 1, 1952, p. 80. Emphasis added.

5) *The Watchtower*, Aug. 1, 2001, p. 14. Emphasis added.

6) *The Watchtower*, Jan. 15, 1983, p. 22. Emphasis added.

we know the way of the truth had it not been
for the guidance from the organization? Really, can we get along without the direction of
God's organization?" No, we cannot![7]

From these statements it is clear that his whole belief
system is grounded upon, not his own thoughts, but what
the Watchtower Society has told him: how to read the Bible
and how to think — within the strict guidelines of what the
Watchtower Society teaches. The only "truth" that matters
to them is what they are told through the Watchtower Society's publications. These are the characteristics of a cult. *In
short, it is mind control.* You now have a clearer understanding how the Witnesses think and why your Bible-based arguments have no effect.

Summary

- Witnesses are taught to "*avoid* independent thinking."

- They are to "*fight against* independent thinking."

- The sum total strategy of the Jehovah's Witnesses
  message is based on two key points:

1. His reliance on the Watchtower Society's
   interpretation of the Bible. "Unless we are in touch
   with this channel of communication that God is
   using, we will not progress along the road to life,
   no matter how much Bible reading we do."[8]

---

7) *The Watchtower*, Jan. 15, 1983, p. 27. Emphasis added.
8) *The Watchtower*, Dec. 1, 1981, p. 27. Emphasis added.

2. His inability to think on his own and present a "gospel" within the strict guidelines of The Watchtower Society. Really, can we get along without the direction of God's organization?' No, we cannot![9]

Just as a sinner needs to repent from sin before he can accept Jesus as Saviour and Lord, the Jehovah's Witness must first come to a place of rejecting the *authority* and *message* of The Watchtower Society.

Since he has been taught to avoid and fight against independent thinking, your attempts to witness will continue to face the obstacle of what he has given himself to trusting —The Watchtower's authority and not the pagan message he believes *you* have.

Your challenge is to destroy his confidence in the Watchtower organization and its publications. Once you are able to help him truly acknowledge that the Watchtower Society is a false prophet, you are on your way to leading one of Jehovah's Witnesses out of the clutches of the Watchtower Society and into the hands of our loving Saviour.

Your strategy is not to confront him with the Bible; but to confront the source that feeds him what he believes to be God's message.

---

9) *The Watchtower*, Jan. 15, 1983, p. 27. Emphasis added.

CHAPTER 2

The Watchtower's Purpose and Eternal Value

Similar to door-to-door salesmen, the Jehovah's Witnesses are expert in defending their "product" — the message of The Watchtower Society. Because they do not know the religious persuasion of their prospective convert in their door-to-door activities, they are required to understand every major religion they may encounter.

Whether the householder is Protestant, Catholic, Baha'i, Mormon, Buddhist, Secular Humanist or Hindu, the Witness is thoroughly trained in presenting an effective witness in an attempt to win the householder to "the ark of The Watchtower Society."

To assist in their preaching efforts, the Witnesses rehearse a series of techniques that train them how to convince and win those of other faiths to the Watchtower Society. Other than their *Watchtower* and *Awake!* magazines, they may carry a few other books which prepare the Witnesses to successfully confront any argument they may face.

Three of these books may be *Reasoning from the Scriptures, Knowledge that Leads to Everlasting Life* and *What Does the Bible Really Teach?*

The first is a topical book the Witnesses use to counter literally dozens of objections and/or questions such as theology, politics, holidays, reincarnation and evolution — issues which the householder may bring up in objecting to religion or even The Watchtower Society itself.

The *Knowledge* book and *What Does the Bible Really Teach?* are doctrinal books used to teach potential converts. They challenge the beliefs of the householder and are designed to persuade the individual that the Watchtower Society is truly God's organization — the true religion. They have proven to be very successful.

Any Biblical points you may use to counter Watchtower theology will be viewed as offensive because the arguments are "pagan" in origin. They may leave your doorstep or stand there and insist on making their point. This is where you are in danger of arguing. Once the arguing starts, an effective witness will most always be lost.

Keep in mind: they believe that *they* have the truth and

are there to teach *you* — not the other way around. They are well trained to be in complete control.

By using these three books, the Witnesses come well pre-pared with Watchtower Society answers for those they en-counter. *However, without the authority of their publications, the Witnesses are rendered powerless and are at your mercy.*

It is the authority of their publications that is your en-emy, not the individual Jehovah's Witness. To be effective in witnessing to these people it is critical that you understand this. For then, you will recognize that **their confidence in their literature is their vulnerability.**

Summary

- Jehovah's Witnesses are expert in defending their "product," the message of The Watchtower Society.

- The Witnesses rehearse a series of techniques to win those of other faiths to their religion.

- Three books Witnesses use are *Reasoning from the Scriptures, Knowledge that Leads to Everlasting Life* and *What Does the Bible Really Teach?*

- Any Biblical points you may use to counter Watchtower theology will be viewed as offensive.

- When arguing starts, an effective witness will *always* be lost.

- If you can destroy their confidence in the authority of their publications, they will be rendered powerless.

How The Watchtower Trains Jehovah's Witnesses

> "It's all there," Father replied. "Just play the record, read the questions, have the householder read the answers, and then read the scriptures."[1]

In the early days, "Bible Students" (early Jehovah's Witnesses) went door-to-door with a portable record player, playing the Watchtower's message on vinyl records. Each record included a series of questions which were directed to the householder from a small Watchtower-published card.

As you read the *Watchtower* quote above, note that the answer is given *before* the scripture is read. The Watchtower Society has already decided for the reader the interpretation in the form of the answer(s) before the scripture is quoted.

This is mind control in its early stages… and you as a potential convert don't even know it's happening!

Today, this technique is still used at the Kingdom Hall Watchtower meetings. A question is read from *The Watchtower*, and the Witness answers what the Society has already provided by reading the "answer" from *The Watchtower*.

Jehovah's Witnesses are not allowed to answer questions based on their own understanding of what was read. In blind obedience, they give answers that have been provided for them — word-for-word in *The Watchtower*. These are the same answers they give to you.

---

1) *The Watchtower*, March 1, 1998, p. 21. Emphasis added.

What is the significance of *The Watchtower* to the Jehovah's Witness? Remember: they base their salvation on "truth" as they understand the scriptures through the lens of the Society's interpretations. It is *these same publications* they will use in an attempt to convert you or those you love.

Summary

- *The Watchtower* is still used in today's Watchtower meetings, and they, not scripture, give the Witnesses all their answers.

- Jehovah's Witnesses are not allowed to answer any questions outside of what The Watchtower Society supplies. In their blind obedience their answers have been provided for them — word-for-word from *The Watchtower.*

- These are the same answers they will give to you.

Their Primary Book for Study

In the book *Reasoning from the Scriptures,* the Watchtower gave this definition of Jehovah's Witnesses:

> The worldwide Christian society of people who actively bear witness regarding Jehovah God and his purposes affecting mankind. *They base their beliefs solely on the Bible.*[2]

But to Jehovah's Witnesses, the Bible is a mysterious book

2) *Reasoning from the Scriptures*, 1985, 1989 editions, p. 199. Emphasis added.

which can only be revealed by The Watchtower. Here are some questions you can ask to help the Jehovah's Witness understand this inconsistency:

Christian: Is there harm in reading the Bible without the aid of *The Watchtower?*

If they answer "Yes," then ask something like this:

Christian: Is it because one has to read *The Watchtower* to interpret the Bible or become one of Jehovah's Witnesses?

Christian: Is the Bible **that** deceptive without interpretations of *The Watchtower?*

In 1971, *The Watchtower* admitted that the Bible should be mankind's primary textbook for study.

> Is it not obvious why *this Book of books should be mankind's primary textbook for study?* Christians, above all, are keenly concerned about investigating this Book that is authored by the One to whom God's Son said: "Your word is truth."[3]

Although *The Watchtower* said the Bible *should* be mankind's primary textbook for study, the Watchtower Society also said:

> In 1982 the book *You Can Live Forever in Paradise on Earth* became the primary book used in conducting Bible studies.[4]

---

3) *The Watchtower*, April 15, 1971, p. 230. Emphasis added.
4) *The Watchtower*, Jan 15, 1997, p. 25. Emphasis added.

The October 1982 issue of *Our Kingdom Ministry* said:

> In the some 20 years that 'Let God Be True'
> was our *primary study book*...[5]

These statements clearly show that *the Bible is **not** their book for primary study.* The Watchtower's publications are the primary source used to interpret scripture.

Remember *The Watchtower's* own words:

> "It's all there," Father replied. "Just play the record, read the questions, have the house-holder read the answers, and then read the scriptures."[6]

Finally, you may ask:

Christian: "Where would you get your beliefs from if you didn't have *The Watchtower?*"

There would be no beliefs! This question is important because it will lead you into the next line of questioning.

Quick Quiz

1. The Jehovah's Witnesses believe the Bible is their book for primary study. True or false?[7]

2. The Watchtower Society uses other "primary study aids" to interpret the Bible. True or false?[8]

---

5) *The Watchtower*, Kingdom Ministry, Oct. 1982, p. 1. Emphasis added.
6) *The Watchtower*, Mar. 1, 1998, p. 21.
7) Answer: False.
8) Answer: True.

   3. If not for their study aids, they would have no
     interpretation or message. True or false?[9]

By asking the numbered questions, your focus is to guide the Witness away from appealing to The Watchtower Society as a source of authority.

At this point you may continue to ask which has more purpose and value to you: The Bible or *The Watchtower?* This is a very important question because you may be on your way to the start of a successful witness.

Challenging and Undermining
The Watchtower Society's Message

Without The Watchtower Society, the Jehovah's Witnesses would have no message. This section will challenge the authority of The Watchtower Society and undermine its purpose and eternal value.

I have included a series of non-threatening, yet thought-provoking questions you can ask the Jehovah's Witnesses. The answers will not be found in their literature, so they will have nothing to appeal to and you will catch them off guard. *This will force them to think for themselves.*

These questions are critical because they avoid the "flash point" that starts arguments: the Bible. Remember: it is pointless to argue Bible passages because of *their dependence on the Watchtower Society's interpretation* of scripture. These questions will help you avoid full-blown arguments and

---

9) Answer: True.

will plant seeds of doubt and undermine the authority of The Watchtower Society

Beliefs Based Solely on the Bible?

At the onset of one meeting I had with a Jehovah's Witness, he took control and ran me from scripture to scripture to prove that God's name is Jehovah.

Christian: Why is knowing God's name so important?

JW: (No answer.)

The Witness only took me from scripture to scripture to try and justify his beliefs. But I stayed away from the Bible and focused on the *source* of his beliefs.

Christian: How did you come to know these truths?

JW: By reading the Bible.

Christian: Don't you use study aids, like *The Watchtower?*

JW: Yes.

Christian: I am convinced that what you are telling me is **not** based upon the Bible, but on what you have read in *The Watchtower*, someone else's interpretation of the Bible. Let me ask you: had it not been for *The Watchtower,* what would your message be to me today?

JW: No answer.

The fact is, *there would be no message without The Watchtower Society!* This opens the door to implementing a plan. You must destroy their line of communication from

The Watchtower Society by asking effective and thought-provoking questions. Your goal is to destroy his confidence in The Watchtower's authority, *not to argue theology.*

Quick Quiz

1. What is the message of the Jehovah's Witness without The Watchtower Society?[10]

2. What is the "flash point" of arguments between Jehovah's Witnesses and Christians? Why?[11]

3. Why must you ask Jehovah's Witnesses questions regarding the authority of The Watchtower?[12]

Your strategy for witnessing to Jehovah's Witnesses is simple: avoid theology and arguments, and focus on destroying their line of communication —The Watchtower Society.

Getting the Witness to Question the Need for The Watchtower Society

Earlier, I quoted the Watchtower's definition of "Jehovah's Witnesses." The last sentence read, "They base their beliefs solely on the Bible." This is not true.

The dictionary defines the word *solely* as "alone; without others." If Jehovah's Witnesses "base their beliefs solely on the Bible," then you should ask why they need study aids such as *The Watchtower.*

---

10) There is no message without *The Watchtower.*
11) The Bible, because it starts arguments.
12) To destroy the authority of *The Watchtower* in their eyes.

Their statement is a lie! The Witnesses base their beliefs on the "Biblical interpretation" of *The Watchtower*. Without it, they have no interpretation and no message.

Want to prove your case? Show the Witnesses they have elevated The Watchtower Society above the Word of God by asking the following questions:

Christian: What would your life be without The Watchtower Society? Why?

Christian: What would life be like without Jesus?

Christian: Which loss would be greater? Why?

Christian: According to John 14:6, Jesus stated that He is "the way, the truth, and the life." What qualifications does the Watchtower Society have that equals Jesus' claim?

Christian: Do you find your spiritual convictions and life's purpose from Jesus or The Watchtower Society? Why?

Christian: If Jesus' claim in John 14:6 is true, then why do you need The Watchtower Society?

Christian: If The Watchtower Society really is God's spokesperson, which is the greatest of all gifts to mankind, Jesus or The Watchtower Society? Why?

WARNING:
Do not bombard the Witness with these questions!

Allow him to ***think*** about what was asked so your questions can "sink in." Please don't let the Witness change the subject. They are skillful at this. Once he changes subjects, you are on his playing field and you have lost complete control of the conversation and are at his mercy.

If you feel in your spirit you are not content with his answers you may ask **one or more** of these questions:

Christian: Would you have an answer to my questions if you did not have *The Watchtower?*

Christian: Are your answers based upon the Bible alone, or what you read in *The Watchtower?*

Christian: How did you arrive at what you believe is true, on your own or from *The Watchtower?*

Use your own personality and style as you ask these questions. They are designed to make the Witness question the purpose and eternal value of *The Watchtower* and to recognize that he depends on it more than the written words of God. Your questions set the foundation for even more critical questions.

Is The Watchtower Inspired of God?

… The Watchtower Society has also said that the fact that some have Jehovah's spirit "does **not** mean those now serving as Jehovah's witnesses are **inspired.** It does **not** mean that the writings in this magazine, *The Watchtower,* are **inspired** and **infallible** and **without mistakes.**"[13]

13) *Awake!* Magazine, Mar. 22, 1993, p. 4. Emphasis added.

... The brothers preparing these publications are **not infallible**. Their writings are **not inspired** as are those of Paul and the other Bible writers.[14]

... However, The Watchtower does **not** claim to be **inspired** in its utterances, nor is it dogmatic.[15] (See Figure 1.)

By these statements it is clear: ***The Watchtower is not inspired, and neither are its writers****. This is a critical issue.*

The Witnesses will never bring up the issue of "inspiration" in their door-to-door work, nor will they expect you to bring it up. This will be to your advantage. The question of inspiration is not discussed in their literature (which provides their pre-prepared answers).

But you *must* bring up this issue, and he will be caught off guard. Show him the quotes we just showed you. The Jehovah's Witness will be stuck.

Now you will need to remind him that the Word of God **is inspired.** (See II Timothy 3:16)

This issue raises three questions you need to ask:

1. Since the Bible **is** the inspired Word of God what is its purpose and eternal value to the Witnesses?

2. If *The Watchtower* is **not** inspired like the Bible, what is its purpose and eternal value?

---

14) *Awake!* Magazine, Mar. 22, 1993, p. 4. Emphasis added.
15) *The Watchtower*, Aug. 15, 1950, p. 263.

3. If *The Watchtower* is **not** inspired by Jehovah, to what will the Witness appeal as his authority?

The Watchtower does not represent the voice or authority of God because it is not inspired by Him. It has neither eternal purpose nor value. It is useless to save you from hell, forgive your sins or prepare you for heaven.

NOTE

To be better prepared, it is best to write these questions down and study them. Feel free to write them down in your own words. This way, they will not sound as if they are rehearsed. After all, when they are your own questions you are better prepared and will be much more confident in your witness.

False Watchtower Prophecies

False prophecies by *The Watchtower* give further evidence that it is not inspired by Jehovah God.

> Jehovah's Witnesses, in their eagerness for Jesus' second coming have suggested dates that turned out to be incorrect.

> **Never in these instances,** however, **did they presume to originate predictions in the name of Jehovah. Never did they say,** 'These are the words of Jehovah.'[16] (See Figure 2.)

The predictions, which the Society admits making, were

16) *Awake!* Magazine, Mar. 22, 1993, p. 4. Emphasis added.

Br AUGUST 15, 1950   The WATCHTOWER   263

speak G...nough to peer into the future, by use of ...'s way, recorded inspired prophecy. It views mod- n Jehov...rn conditions and events in the light of litions, s...God's Word, being receptive to Jehovah's ters and...message, and quick to declare his truths inquenc...nd judgments. Jehovah commands the nsider t...watchman class to "call aloud, hold not reement...ack, lift up your voice like a trumpet; d world...how my people their transgression". (Isa. n of go...8: 1, *An Amer. Trans.*) As a voice for 1, then...the watchman class, *The Watchtower* has that su...rumpeted forth the sins of thos... of the...ng to serve God, and at pres... up : 1-6)...ss voice in thirty languag... ...eard ses of...hroughout the nations... e, cruel...Viewed in this...may be said that iersom...he *Watchto*...ds as a watchman on world...tlookout...lert to what is going on, hey do...ake...te signs that warn of danger, fable...tick to point the way to life in a new ng the...rld. It heralds the news of Jehovah's see t...gdom established by Christ's enthrone- Matt....nt in heaven, warns that we live in the eyes...days of this old world, cries out that perceiv...ovah's battle of Armageddon comes on att. 1...ce, feeds the kingdom joint-heirs with are...ritual food, cheers men of good will with will...ious prospects of eternal life in a para- rld of...earth, and comforts us with the resur- ...ion promise for the dead. All this it ...with confident ring in its voice, be- MA...e its words find their foundation in his t...ith's Word. It is not a blind or dumb ?...chman, but tries to keep in tune with offic...by searching his Word and being re- Just...ive to his guidance, with eyes always ntage...to prophecy so that it knows what to *The W*...for in world events, so that it under- pinnacle...s the significance of what it sees. It s Word...not privately interpret prophecy, but party...attention to physical facts, sets them pagand...side prophecy, and you see for your- es fro...ow well the two match, how accurate- arp v...ovah interprets his own prophecy. shortsight...et. 1: 20, 21. and...far

Hence the purpose of this magazine is to keep sharp and faithful focus on Bible truth, on world happenings that may fulfill prophecies, and on religious news generally. Sometimes it will tear down religious falsehoods, that Bible truth may be built up in their stead. Such two-way work is Scripturally commanded, and is beneficial for all persons of right heart condition. (Jer. 1: 10; Heb. 12: 5-13) However, *The Watchtower* does not claim to be inspired in its utterances, nor is it dogmatic. It invites careful and critical examination of its contents in the light of the Scriptures. Its purpose is to aid others to know Jehovah and his purposes toward mankind, and to announce Christ's established kingdom as our only hope.

Jehovah God is the Teacher of his people, but we must "be on the watch" to catch his instruction. We must "not sleep like the rest of men, but be wakeful and sober". To those who do slumber the wakeful ones must cry, "It is high time to awake!" (Isa. 54: 13; Rom. 13: 11; 1 Cor. 16: 13, *An Amer. Trans.*; 1 Thess. 5: 6, *Moffatt*) If you have been asleep to the signs of the times, not watching world developments in the light of Bible prophecies, then you must obey the command to wake up and watch. Let *The Watchtower* help you heed such admonition that leads to life, for that is its purpose.

Faithfully living up to its name and purpose, *The Watchtower* does stand alone in its field, and its value is unmeasurable in money. It declares God's wisdom, which is "better than rubies; and all the things that may be desired are not to be compared to it". Such wisdom "is a tree of life". *The Watchtower* beckons you to lay hold upon that wisdom, and gain life in a new world without end.—Prov. 3: 13-18; 8: 10, 11; Eph. 3: 21.

Figure 1 The Watchtower, August 15, 1950, p. 263

not authorized by Jehovah God. In other words, they were **not inspired**. The Watchtower Society was not just in error; they were not even inspired to begin with.

Summary

- Learn these two quotes:

  "The brothers preparing these publications are not infallible. **Their writings are not inspired** as are those of Paul and the other Bible writers."[17]

  "It does not mean that the writings in this magazine *The Watchtower* are inspired and infallible and without mistakes."[18]

- The Watchtower defines inspiration as "The quality or state of being moved by or produced under the direction of a spirit from a superhuman source."[19]

- Is the Bible inspired? **Yes.** (See 2 Timothy 3:16)

- Is *The Watchtower* inspired? **No.**[20]

- If *The Watchtower* is not inspired, then it is not "being moved by or produced under the direction of a spirit from a superhuman source" (Jehovah) by those "brothers" who prepare the publications.

---

17) *Awake!* Magazine, Mar. 22, 1993, p. 4. Emphasis added.
18) *Awake!* Magazine, Mar. 22, 1993, p. 4. Emphasis added.
19) *Insight on the Scriptures*, Vol. 1, 1988, p. 1202.
20) See *Awake!* Magazine, Mar. 22, 1993, p. 4; and *The Watchtower*, Aug. 15, 1950, p. 263.

words do not come true, they should not be viewed as false prophets such as those warned against at Deuteronomy 18:20-22. In their human fallibility...

en. Several other doomsday groups made similar predictions.

The flood of false alarms is unfortunate.

Undeterred... to have been... year 2000 a... of the end of th... of December 5... titled "Millenn... ate, the End Is... proaching, var... that Jesus is co... "a time of trou... fore." At the... est occurrence... where the Miss... dicted that on... Christ would c...

* Jehovah's Witnesses, in their eagerness for Jesus' second coming, have suggested dates that turned out to be incorrect. Because of this, some have called them false prophets. Never in these instances, however, did they presume to originate predictions 'in the name of Jehovah.' Never did they say, 'These are the words of Jehovah.' *The Watchtower,* the official journal of Jehovah's Witnesses, has said: "We have *not* the gift of prophecy." (January 1883, page 425) "Nor would we have our writings reverenced or regarded as infallible." (December 15, 1896, page 306) *The Watchtower* has also said that the fact that some have Jehovah's spirit "does not mean those now serving as Jehovah's witnesses are inspired. It does not mean that the writings in this magazine *The Watchtower* are inspired and infallible and without mistakes." (May 15, 1947, page 157) *"The Watchtower* does not claim to be inspired in its utterances, nor is it dogmatic." (August 15, 1950, page 263) "The brothers preparing these publications are not infallible. Their writings are not inspired as are those of Paul and the other Bible writers. (2 Tim. 3:16) And so, at times, it has been necessary, as understanding became clearer, to correct views. (Prov. 4:18)"—February 15, 1981, page 19.

* Jehovah's Witne... coming, have sugge... Because of this, som... in these instances... predictions 'in the... 'These are the word... ficial journal of Jeh... the gift of prophecy... we have our writin... (December 15, 1896... that the fact that so... those now serving a... not mean that the writings in this magazine *The Watchtower* are inspired and infallible and without mistakes." (May 15, 1947, page 157) *The Watchtower* does not claim to be inspired in its utterances, nor is it dogmatic." (August 15, 1950, page 263) "The brothers preparing these publications are not infallible. Their writings are not inspired as are those of Paul and the other Bible writers. (2 Tim. 3:16) And so, at times, it has been necessary, as understanding became clearer, to correct views. (Prov. 4:18)"—February 15, 1981, page 19.

see it at the door even when the evidence is insufficient. In our eagerness false alarms may be sounded.

What, then, will distinguish the true warning from the false ones? For the answer, please see the following article.

Awake!®

Why *Awake!* Is Published *Awake!* is for the enlightenment of the entire family. It shows how to cope with today's problems. It reports the news, tells about people in many lands, examines religion and science. But it does more. It probes beneath the surface and points to the real meaning behind current events, yet it always stays politically neutral and does not exalt one race above another. Most important, this magazine builds confidence in the Creator's promise of a peaceful and secure new world before the generation that saw the events of 1914 passes away.

Would you welcome more information? Write Watch Tower at the appropriate address on page 5. This is part of a worldwide Bible educational work that is supported by voluntary donations.

Unless otherwise indicated, *New World Translation of the Holy Scriptures—With References* is used.

Awake! (ISSN 0005-237X) is published semimonthly by Watchtower Bible and Tract Society of New York, Inc., 25 Columbia Heights, Brooklyn, N.Y. 11201. Second-class postage paid at Brooklyn, N.Y., and at additional mailing offices. *Postmaster:* Send address changes to *Awake!* c/o Watchtower, *Wallkill, N.Y. 12589.* Vol. 74, No. 6
Printed in U.S.A.

Figure 2 Awake! Magazine, March 22, 1993 p. 4.

- By their own admission, "Jehovah's Witnesses, in their eagerness for Jesus' second coming have suggested dates that turned out to be incorrect."

- The Watchtower claims, "Never in these instances, however, did they say, 'These are the words of Jehovah.'"

- Because The Watchtower Society did not say that their predictions were the words of Jehovah, what they predicted was not inspired by Jehovah, either.

- So what is the purpose and eternal value of an uninspired publication such as *The Watchtower*, if the events foretold did not come to pass?

Part Two
Creating an Effective Witnessing Strategy

CHAPTER 3

Key Elements to an Effective Witness

You may have a loved one, a close friend or a co-worker who is either thinking of becoming one of Jehovah's Witnesses or is already serving in the organization; and you want quick and easy answers how to present an effective witness to these precious people.

There are three key elements in presenting an anointed and effective witness to the Jehovah's Witnesses.

• **Pray:** seek the Lord's wisdom in your witness. Pray for the individual you are going to witness to.

• **Rehearse:** Write down the questions presented in this book and familiarize yourself by practicing (role playing) using the strategies outlined in this book.

• **Propose:** present your witness to the Jehovah's Witness with gentleness and the love of God. *Do not condemn* him or her.

Implementing Your Witnessing Strategy

The following conversation will give you ideas how to use the topic of "the inspiration of *The Watchtower*" in your witnessing strategy.

This conversation is based upon many conversations I've had with the Witnesses throughout the years. I advise you to read it over a few times. You will see how vitally important it is to avoid using the Bible until they are ready to reject *The Watchtower's* authority.

JW: Good morning. My name is Richard and this is my wife, Sharon. We'd like to leave you with a study guide for the Bible. Would you like a copy? We can come back in the next week or so to discuss what you've read.

Christian: Thank you. Yes, I'd like a copy. May I ask you something? What is the purpose of having a study guide for the Bible?

JW: That is a very good question. The purpose for this magazine is to share important Biblical truths. I take it that you read the Bible?

Christian: Oh yes. I read it for strength, encouragement —you know, to apply God's wisdom in my life. But getting back to my question: why do you use this magazine as a study guide for the Bible?

JW: We offer this study guide because we are confident that *The Watchtower* reveals Biblical truths hidden from mankind.

Christian: If that is true, then *The Watchtower* must be inspired, just like the Bible is. Is it inspired?

JW: Well, *The Watchtower* is the instrument that we believe God uses to reveal to us His truths.

Christian: Okay, but is *The Watchtower* inspired?

JW: I don't understand your question.

Christian: The Bible says that all scripture is inspired of God. Do you believe that?

JW: Yes.

Christian: If the Bible is inspired, how did it come to be inspired? In other words, what does "inspiration" mean?

JW: I don't see the point of this conversation.

Christian: You are here in my neighborhood because you believe you have an important message for me, don't you? If you want me to join your religion, don't I have the liberty to check out what you are offering me? Shouldn't everyone take the liberty to investigate what they may eventually join their hearts to, if that ends up being the case?

JW: Well, yes. But...

Christian: Didn't you ask questions about this faith before you joined?

JW: Yes.

Christian: Well, here's my question to you: is *The Watchtower* inspired the same way the scriptures are?

JW: Well...

JW #2: Let me answer that question. Why do you need to know? Why are you so adamant with this question?

Christian: Like you, I also am a student of the Bible; and I do not take anything at face value — particularly when it comes to my eternal future. So please answer me: is *The Watchtower* inspired? It's important to me.

JW #2: No. It is not inspired. Is that the answer you wanted to hear?

Christian: It's not what I "wanted to hear." I just want a straightforward, honest answer. It's important to me to know the truth, just like knowing your truth is important to you.

JW: Okay, now that we all know that *The Watchtower* is not inspired, now what?

Christian: Are you making light of my question, or are you being honest?

JW: (No answer.)

Christian: I read my Bible every day knowing and believing it is God's inspired Word to me; and you are asking me to read a study aid that is not inspired. How can an uninspired publication reveal the truth, when the truth is already inspired in the Bible?

JW: And your point is...

Christian: Inspiration has to do with receiving messages and direction from God Himself, right? And if the Bible is inspired, and *The Watchtower* is not, which has greater eternal purpose and value?

JW #2: Which has the greater value?

Christian: Let me say it another way: I am holding here *The Watchtower* that you gave me. May I borrow your Bible? Thank you. Now I am holding the Bible. Because the Bible is inspired and *The Watchtower* is not, upon which should I place more value: the inspired Bible or this *Watchtower*, which you just said is **not** inspired?

JW: Well, that's not what we came to discuss today.

Christian: Then what did you come here to discuss?

JW #2: Uh...we were just handing out *Watchtowers*.

Christian: So you were handing out *Watchtowers*, which contain an uninspired message? Do you see my concern?

JW #2: Like I said, we were just here in the neighborhood passing out *Watchtowers*... and proclaiming God's kingdom and hope to those who will hear.

Christian: So are you saying that this proclamation came from… what, the *Watchtowers* you are handing out? Am I to understand that your message is from an uninspired *Watchtower* and not from the inspired Bible?

JW: You have it wrong. We do teach from the Bible.

Christian: Then here is your *Watchtower* along with its uninspired message. I'll stay with my Bible. How do you know that an uninspired magazine is revealing truth? If you say you teach from the Bible, hand out Bibles and not *The Watchtower*. But if *The Watchtower* truly is God's word to mankind, can you give me back *The Watchtower* with a clear conscience, knowing that it is an uninspired study aid?

Christian: I see in your hands a Bible and a *Watchtower*. Were you to lose one or the other, which would be the greater loss?

JW: (No answer.)

Christian: I have three questions I would like you to think about: What would your life be like without *The Watchtower?* What would life be like without Jesus? Which loss would be greater?

JW: You raise some valid points, but we must remain faithful to what we hold to be truth.

Christian: Which truth? The truth of the Bible, or from an uninspired *Watchtower?* If I must believe an inspired message over one that is not inspired, which would be the wiser choice? Please help me out here. You said you were going door to door handing out *Watchtowers* and its message. What is *The Watchtower's* message?

JW #2: Dare I answer? You know, I respect your opinions and have listened to what you had to say, but our message is...well, our message is...

Christian: ...**not** inspired, according to your own words. I would hope that your message will one day be taken from this inspired Book called the Bible. I hope you will come to the point where you are honest with yourself and reconsider delivering a message that has **never** originated with God, and use His inspired Word instead.

Note that in my witnessing I did not quote scriptural passages to make my points. I used simple logic based upon comparing the purpose and eternal value of the Bible to the uninspired *Watchtower.* My goal was to get the Witnesses to **think**: which has the greater eternal purpose and value, the Bible or *The Watchtower?*

Do you understand the purpose of this witnessing strategy instead of going toe-to-toe arguing scripture? Your goal is to weaken the source of the Jehovah's Witnesses' beliefs —The Watchtower Society. Once the supply line fails, their trust in the Watchtower Society will fail also.

The Witnesses are well-prepared for a Biblical confrontation. That is what they always expect; *but they will not expect anyone to address the source that feeds them.* They have no defense against the evidence that *The Watchtower* is not inspired.

These first three chapters raise important questions; but The Watchtower Society has much to do to explain other issues it has taught from their uninspired work. The following chapters will illustrate further problems with the uninspired *Watchtower.* These are problems you can also address in your witnessing strategy.

Regardless what The Watchtower Society says now or in the future, its message will forever be *uninspired.*

If the Watchtower Society were to one day change its position and claim to be inspired, then everything written in *The Watchtower* from the first *Watchtower* magazine (July, 1879) to present day would no longer be valid theology because it was all uninspired.

This means that the Jehovah's Witnesses would be forced to re-structure everything they were taught under the un-inspired Watchtower and start a new belief structure beginning with any new "inspired" messages.

Any such change would not only affect their entire theology base but the name *Jehovah's Witnesses* as well, which has separated them from Christianity.

Why? The name Jehovah's Witnesses was given to them in 1931 – during the time when *The Watchtower* was believed to never have been inspired. If the Watchtower Society were to one day claim inspiration, what would their new name be?

The fact is that the Watchtower Society can never claim to be inspired. Any new "inspired" theology would have a negative effect on millions of Jehovah's Witnesses worldwide, and would risk the collapse of the entire Watchtower organization.

CHAPTER 4

Did Jesus Die on a Cross?

Early *Watchtower* publications taught that Jesus died on a cross. (See Figure 3). However, that changed during the leadership of Joseph Franklin Rutherford, second President of the Watchtower Bible and Tract Society.

Watchtower artist renderings eventually showed Jesus nailed to a *torture stake*. (See Figure 4.) This is accepted today by all Jehovah's Witnesses, and is one of the most common statements a Jehovah's Witness makes:

> We know that Jesus was nailed to the torture stake.[1]

---

1) *The Watchtower*, Jan. 15, 1966, p. 63.

Figure 3 from *Life* by J.F. Rutherford (Brooklyn, NY: International Bible Students Association, Watchtower Bible and Tract Society), 1929, p. 198.

According to *The Watchtower,* a torture stake is a single standing pole with no cross beam, and just a *single nail* that pierced both of Jesus' hands above His head. This may seem a minor point, but it will prove to be critical.

While artist's rendering of Jesus on the *torture stake* shows **both** of his hands being pierced with **one** nail, on the same page of this article *The Watchtower* states:

> In one instance, he invited Thomas to inspect the wounds inflicted in his hands by means of the **nails**. (John 20:19-29).[2]

The Watchtower made two contradictory statements. First it said that Jesus was nailed to a *torture stake*, which would require only **one** nail. But the same article mentioned "**wounds** inflicted in his hands by means of the **nails** (John 20:19-29)." Is it one nail or two?

Indecision in The Watchtower

In 1966, The Watchtower Society was certain that Jesus was fastened by *a nail* to a *torture stake*; however, they were *not so sure* in 1987:

> We cannot know precisely where the **nails** pierced him, though it was obviously in the area of his hands. The Scriptural account simply does not provide exact details, nor does it need to.

---

2) *The Watchtower*, Jan. 15, 1966, p. 63. Emphasis added.

Illustrations of Christ on a "torture stake" in Jehovah's Witness materials.

Figure 4a from *The Knowledge That Leads To Everlasting Life,* 1995, p. 67.

Figure 4b from *You Can Live Forever In Paradise On Earth,* 1982, p. 170.

Figure 4c from *My Book of Bible Stories,* 1978, p. 100.

> We thus recognize that depictions of Jesus'
> death in our publications, such as you see on
> page 24, *are merely reasonable artistic render-*
> *ings* of the scene, not statements of anatomi-
> cal absolutes.[3]

Nails? I thought He died on a torture stake! And note
that The Watchtower Society continued to state that the
"depictions of Jesus' death" in their publications "are *merely*
reasonable artistic renderings of the scene."

While in 1966 *The Watchtower* was sure that Jesus died
on a torture stake, they continued to use the plural word
"nails" in the articles. Does this make sense?

The Watchtower also said:

> Any drawings of Jesus on the stake should be
> understood as artist's productions that offer
> merely *a representation based on the limited*
> *facts we have.*[4]

Although today's *Watchtower* publications picture Jesus
on the torture stake, the reader is **now** told that these pic-
tures are merely a *representation* based on the limited facts.

Does this sound like absolute truth to you? Can the
Watchtower Society's message on the manner of Jesus' death
be fully trusted as absolute truth?

Even after the Watchtower Society made these state-

---

3) *The Watchtower*, Aug. 15, 1987, p. 29. Emphasis added.
4) *The Watchtower*, Apr. 1, 1984, p. 31. Emphasis added.

ments, today's *Watchtower* publications still insist on depicting Jesus on a *torture stake* with a **single** nail. Since they admit they are not inspired, why does a Jehovah's Witness have to believe Jesus died in this manner?

This is important. *The Watchtower's* position *is inconsistent with itself. But more importantly, it disagrees with the Bible!* Is *The Watchtower's* position and evidence definitive and persuasive? Or does The Watchtower Society simply state another *opinion* about how Jesus died?

Questions

1. Did a *torture stake* require one nail or two?
Answer: One nail pierced both hands.

2. Can *The Watchtower* reconcile saying Jesus died on a *torture stake,* and use the plural word "nails?"
Answer: No, they can't.

3. Does the Bible use the word "nail" or "nails?"
Answer: The Bible says "nails." See John 20:25.

4. Because the Bible is inspired, is it safe to accept it *alone* as absolute truth?
Answer: Yes.

5. If *The Watchtower* is not inspired, what scripture supports its teaching of the *torture stake*?
Answer: There is no scriptural support.

6. Is the Watchtower Society certain that Jesus died on a *torture stake?*
Answer: No. It is merely their opinion.

How Does the Bible Say Jesus Died?

In the artist's rendering of Jesus on the *torture stake,* the sign which reads "This is Jesus the King of the Jews," is posted above Jesus' hands. This is in stark contrast to the Biblical account of Jesus' death.

> Also they posted above his head the charge against him, in writing: "This is Jesus the King of the Jews."[5]

You may ask the Witnesses:

Christian: According to the Biblical account of Jesus' death, note that a sign was placed above Jesus' **head** and not His **hands** as seen on a *torture stake.* Is *The Watchtower's* depiction of Jesus' death based upon Biblical truth? If not, upon what is it based?

You may also state:

Christian: The Bible states that the inscription was posted above his **head**. This would mean that His arms were stretched out to each side. *The Watchtower's* interpretation is quite different from the Biblical account. The artist's renderings show the inscription above Jesus' **hands** on the *torture stake*.

Then ask:

Christian: Is this based upon eyewitness accounts as recorded in scripture?

---

5) Matthew 27:37 *New World Translation*, 1984 Edition. Emphasis added.

The Bible quotes the words of Thomas:

> "Except I shall see in his **hands** the print of
> the **nails**, and put my finger into the print of
> the **nails**, and thrust my hand into his side,
> I will not believe" [that Jesus rose from the
> dead.][6]

Again, the plural word "nails" is used.[7] Thomas knew
that Jesus died on a cross, which in the Greek language is
the word *stauros*. Incidentally, the letter "†" in the Greek
alphabet is pronounced "*tau*" – exactly like the sound in
the word *stauros* (cross). Coincidence?

Questions To Ask

1. In the Bible, is the inscription above Jesus'
   head or hands?
   Answer: Head. (Matthew 27:37)

2. In *The Watchtower's* renderings of the *torture stake*
   is the inscription above His head or hands?
   Answer: Hands.

3. Which of these two accounts represents the
   truth, the Bible or The Watchtower Society?
   Answer: The Bible.

4. Should our faith be based on the Bible or The
   Watchtower Society?
   Answer: The Bible.

---

6) See John 20:25.

7) This passage mentions "nails" only in Jesus' hands, not His feet.

Be sure to **write down** these questions in your own words to better prepare your witnessing strategy.

Implementing Your Witnessing Strategy

This conversation is based upon many conversations I've had with Witnesses through years. It will show how to use the topic of "how Jesus died" in your witnessing strategy.

Christian: I was looking at some *Watchtower* literature and noticed something I don't think many Christians know about: the way *The Watchtower* says Jesus died.

JW: Yes. We believe that Jesus died on a *torture stake*, not on a cross.

Christian: I'm sure that your evidence is detailed. Is it?

JW: Yes.

Christian: Well, how sure is The Watchtower Society that Jesus died on a torture stake?

JW: Quite sure.

Christian: Are you saying The Watchtower Society believes that the Bible teaches He died on a torture stake?

JW: Of course. What are you getting at?

Christian: I took a close look at the picture of Jesus nailed to the torture stake, and found that what the scripture said was quite different from the illustrations in *The Watchtower*.

JW: Well, your idea of what you read is your own interpretation.

Christian: So are you saying that the correct interpretation of scripture can **only** be found in *The Watchtower?*

JW: Yes.

Christian: But what if the Bible contradicts *The Watchtower?* Which of the two should I trust?

JW: That depends on the interpretation.

Christian: Okay. Show me a picture of Jesus on the *stake.* Now look at it closely. What do you see?

JW: I see Jesus on a torture stake. Now what?

Christian: Now let's read John 19:24-25 in your Bible.

JW: "But Thomas, one of the twelve, who was called The Twin, was not with them when Jesus came. Consequently the other disciples would say to him: 'We have seen the Lord!' But he said to them: 'Unless I see in his hands the print of the **nails** and stick my finger into the print of the **nails** and stick my hand into his side, I will certainly not believe.'"

JW: What's your point?

Christian: I want you to see the *Bible's* point.

JW: And the Bible says?

Christian: *The Watchtower* clearly shows **one** nail in Jesus' hands, but Thomas used the plural word "**nails**." How many nails are in the artwork fastening Jesus' hands?

JW: One.

Christian: According to what you believe, *The Watchtower* is correct in **every** area of teaching. But the Bible says Thomas wanted to touch the print of the **nails**; but the illustrations only show **one** nail. So which is correct?

JW: (The witness will probably have no answer.)

Christian: Is this *Watchtower* teaching based upon the inspired Bible as John recorded it?

JW: (No answer.)

Christian: I realize that this is a lot to think about. But there is one other point: I also noted one more thing in the artwork.

JW: You know what? You are reading too much into this and "straining at gnats."

Christian: But we're talking about *The Watchtower* contradicting the inspired word of God in the Bible. I wouldn't call that "straining at gnats."

JW: I see your point.

Christian: I also noted that the inscription Pilate ordered to be written was placed above Jesus' **hands** in *The Watchtower's* artwork. Let's take a look.

JW: And?

Christian: The gospel of Matthew records, "Also they posted above his **head** the charge against him, in writing: 'This is Jesus the King of the Jews.' "(Matthew 27:37) Does the artwork show the inscription placed above His **hands** or His **head**?

JW: His hands.

Christian: Does this agree with the Bible?

JW: I need to do some more research into this. I just don't know. You really confused me.

Christian: How did I confuse you? I didn't write or do the artwork in *The Watchtower* and I certainly did not write the Bible. I just want to know how you reconcile *The Watchtower* with the Bible. If you are sincere in researching this further, remember to ask yourself, "Who is telling me the truth: the Bible or *The Watchtower?*"

The Decision for Truth

The purpose of this witnessing strategy is to show that *The Watchtower* ignores what the Bible teaches. This also reveals the Watchtower Society's control over the minds of the Witnesses — even when *The Watchtower* disagrees with the Bible.

I've had Witnesses tell me, "I'd rather die before I believe that!" This attitude is certainly a fine example of the Witnesses willing to defend *The Watchtower*, rather than take to heart the truth of the Bible. Be prepared for them to tell you the same thing.

At this point you must let them know that they are clearly ignoring the truth of God's Word and choosing to trust and believe an *uninspired* Watchtower.

This is where you need to ask the Witness:

Christian: How do you feel about the true value and eternal purpose of the Bible, if you insist on holding onto a Watchtower teaching that contradicts the Bible? You need to make a choice. Who is telling the truth: the Bible or The Watchtower Society?

If the Witness says the Bible is telling the truth, then he needs to decide: "What shall I do with *The Watchtower?*" If he feels that *The Watchtower* is telling the truth, then he needs to decide: "What shall I do with the Bible? And what is its eternal purpose and value for me?" Of course, without the Bible, *The Watchtower* has no message.

Again: write these ideas down in your own words. That will help you remember how to ask the thought-provoking questions designed to destroy his confidence in The Watchtower Society.

CHAPTER 5

Who Resurrected Jesus?

The Word of God does not contradict itself. However, you can make the Bible *appear to* contradict itself, if you wrongly interpret the scriptures. God's Word is infallible and inspired. When read on its own, it blends in complete harmony with itself. It doesn't need man's uninspired and false interpretation.

What about *The Watchtower's* interpretation of Jesus' resurrection? As you will see, The Watchtower Society makes the scriptures seem to contradict themselves, but their interpretation cannot be reconciled with the Bible.

For Jehovah's Witnesses to believe that the Bible contains

no contradiction, they must read and understand the Bible *without* the interpretation of the Watchtower Society. Then they will see how the Bible blends harmoniously.

Earlier, I stated that it was futile to bring up Biblical passages in your witnessing. However, your purpose in asking who resurrected Jesus in this chapter is to *identify the One Who resurrected Jesus*. In doing this, you will only be interested in three Watchtower articles —which have three different views. And you are only interested in asking them which Watchtower article is supposed to be true.

Remember: the Jehovah's Witnesses have much more respect for The Watchtower Society than the Bible. Why? Because without The Watchtower Society, Jehovah's Witnesses have *no idea* what the Bible is saying.

Jehovah God Resurrected Jesus

An example of *The Watchtower's* interpretation of scriptures is the identity of the One Who resurrected Jesus from the dead. According to the inspired scriptures, God raised Jesus from the dead.

> For if you publicly declare that 'word in your own mouth,' that Jesus is Lord and exercise faith in your heart that **God raised him up from the dead**, you will be saved.[1]

You may ask:

---

1) Romans 10:9 *New World Translation* (1984 Edition). Emphasis added.

Christian: According to *The Watchtower's* interpretation of Romans 10:9, Who resurrected Jesus?

JW: God.

Christian: According to the Witnesses, Who is God?

JW: JEHOVAH.

Christian: Is anyone else identified in this scripture Who resurrected Jesus?

JW: No.

Amazingly, *The Watchtower* also agrees with scripture:

> "Rather, he [Jesus] lay unconscious in death for three days until **God resurrected** him."[2]

Christian: Is it safe to say that, according to Romans 10:9 in the inspired scripture, Jehovah God raised Jesus from the dead?

JW: Yes.

And the only "God" The Watchtower Society recognizes as the true God is Jehovah God — God the Father.

You have now gotten the Witness to admit that Jehovah God raised Jesus.

Jesus' Role in His Own Resurrection

In an article titled "Jesus' Own Words," *The Watchtower* quoted Jesus as saying, "'Break down this temple, and in

---

2) *The Watchtower*, June 15, 1994, p. 6. Emphasis added.

three days I will raise it up.' John adds: He was talking about the temple of his body."[3]

Christian: According to this Watchtower article, Who resurrected Jesus?

They may answer: Jesus did.

But wait! How does a Jehovah's Witness reconcile the above Watchtower teaching that **Jesus** raised up his **own** body with the June 15, 1994 *Watchtower* and Romans 10:9, that say **Jehovah God** raised Jesus from the dead? (You might ask them to write down this issue of *The Watchtower* so they may see it for themselves).

Christian: If this *Watchtower* says that only Jehovah God raised Jesus from the dead, then this *Watchtower* article and the scriptures it quoted contradict the other *Watchtower* article and its scripture quotes.

Christian: Who is telling the truth: The Watchtower Society or God's inspired Word?

If the Witness says "The Bible," then inform him that the Watchtower Society has no authority to interpret scripture and it cannot be trusted because of this contradicting view.

Either way, you have now gotten the Witness to admit that Jesus raised Himself from the dead, *and* Jehovah God raised Jesus from the dead.

---

3) *The Watchtower*, Apr. 15, 1978, p. 27. See John 2:19-21.

The Holy Spirit's Role in Jesus' Resurrection

But this is not all. There is one more *Watchtower* article and scripture the Witness must reconcile with the other two articles and scriptures if *The Watchtower* truly is a study aid to the Bible and represents truth:

> **...results of Jehovah God's spirit in opera-tion:** (1) Creation - Genesis 1:2; Psalm104:30; (2) Birth of Jesus - Matthew 1:18; (3) **Resur-rection of Jesus**- Romans 8:11...)[4]

Christian: According to this *Watchtower* article and Romans 8:11, Who resurrected Jesus?

JW: Jehovah God's spirit.

The Watchtower and its interpretations leave its readers wondering: exactly who resurrected Jesus?

The Witness does not believe in the Trinity,[5] but he may want to discuss it at this point. You must remind him:

Christian: I am not interested in discussing the Trinity. *My sole interest is in knowing Who resurrected Jesus.*

JW: Why?

Christian: Because *The Watchtower* has three different views.

---

4) *The Watchtowe*r, June 15, 1966, p. 359. Emphasis added.
5) Jehovah's Witnesses do not understand the Godhead, so they do not know that the Father, Son and Holy Ghost are one God. They teach that there is only Jehovah God, not the Son or Spirit. These scriptures do not contradict each other, but to a Jehovah's Witness, they will seem to.

This is the point you must establish.

The Witness not only needs to reconcile the scriptures according to *The Watchtower's* interpretation, but also to conclude **which** *Watchtower* view is correct.

Remember, if he chooses one view, then the other two views are wrong. And if the other views are wrong, then the Bible contradicts itself. Why? Remind the Witness that he believes *The Watchtower* is a study aid to the Bible.

This is critical. By citing scripture *The Watchtower* has accidentally taught something contradicting what the Witness has been taught before.

Christian: So my first question is, "Which of the three contradictory *Watchtower* statements should I believe?"

Christian: And my second question is, "Should I believe Watchtower statements that directly contradict the Bible?"

This clearly shows the danger of letting an uninspired publication interpret the scriptures for you. The Witness must decide which has more purpose and eternal value and to what he should give his allegiance: the uninspired *Watchtower* or the Bible?

If he reads the Bible, without *The Watchtower* to interpret it, he will **know** Who resurrected Jesus.

Though you have gotten him to see that Jehovah God, Jesus and God's Spirit raised Jesus, do not discuss the doctrine of the Trinity. It is **highly offensive** to them and you may lose your effective witness.

Summary

- The Bible teaches in Roman 10:9 that God [Jehovah] resurrected Jesus from the dead.

- *The Watchtower* agrees with the Bible.[6]

- The Bible quotes Jesus as saying he would resurrect the Temple of His body.[7]

- *The Watchtower* agrees with the Bible.[8]

- The Bible is used to support the teaching that Jehovah God's Spirit resurrected Jesus.[9]

- *The Watchtower* agrees with the Bible.[10]

- For a Jehovah's Witness, only one of these *Watchtower* positions can be true. Which one is it?

Christian: You as a Witness must decide. Which has more purpose and eternal value, and to which you will give your allegiance: the uninspired *Watchtower*, or the inspired Bible?

---

6) *The Watch*tower, June. 15, 1994, p. 6.

7) John 2:19-21.

8) *The Watchtower*, April 15, 1978, p. 27.

9) Romans 8:11. See also 1 Peter 3:18.

10) *The Watchtower*, June 15, 1966, p. 359.

Part Three

What Happens After They Are Saved?

CHAPTER 6

Cost of Leaving The Watchtower

The Witness you will be sharing this information with will have quite a bit to think about. After all, everything he has held near and dear to him has been challenged and possibly compromised.

This is a critical place for you and him. Why?

I remember meeting with a veteran 27-year Jehovah's Witness who was on the verge of converting her fiancé to become one of Jehovah's Witnesses.

I went over a few witnessing points by questioning the authority of the Watchtower, as outlined in this book. I admit they both were "difficult to deal with." Finally, there was a moment when I perceived a weakness in a position they were attempting to get out of. They failed and they knew it —and so did I.

Without any warning, the man stood up and started screaming at me and his fiancé:

> "They lied to us, honey! They lied to us! What
> are we going to do?"

She looked at him, then at me, with tears flowing down her cheeks.

"*Now* what are we going to do?" he screamed over and over.

I sat there watching this whole scene unfold before me, waiting for them to get this shock out of their system.

At this point, once the Witness recognizes the Watchtower Society is not God's spokesperson on earth, you have reached the most critical point of your ministry.

Now that he is convinced of the errors of The Watchtower Society, will he actually leave his faith? And if he does, what will your role be in his life?

The Trauma of Shattered Faith

Once you lead one of Jehovah's Witnesses out of the Watchtower organization your challenge has just begun.

Many who exit the Watchtower on their own never again involve themselves with "religion" – of any kind. Many become agnostic or atheists. Many have suicidal thoughts.

Some succumb to those thoughts. Thankfully, there are those who, in time, work out the trauma of leaving the Watchtower organization and live meaningful lives.

Many publications deal with ministering to Jehovah's Witnesses; but very few address the trauma of those who exit the Watchtower organization. After all, they feel that the god they served deceived and used them. They are now left holding the broken pieces of their lives that once existed in The Watchtower Society.

Consider your own walk with Christ. You treasure your pastor, your church leadership, and God's Word. You treasure all that Jesus is and what He means to you, and His sacrifice on your behalf. You weep in your worship as you thank Him for His love for you. Your faith is the full measure of your life. Every waking moment is spent with the Lord —your Redeemer.

What if you suddenly found that everything you trusted in was based on speculation, deception and fiction; and the evidence was irrefutable?

To whom would you give your allegiance? Would you ever have faith again? This is the very real dilemma the Witness faces once he realizes the truth about the Watchtower.

The man I met with on that day asked me a very important question:

> "Jehovah has failed me! What guarantee can you give me the God which you say you serve won't fail me too?"

Can you understand the spirit in which he asked this question? His faith and trust in his god were totally shattered. The loss of this religion leaves a deep wound in the heart, like one who has lost a loved one in death. The trauma can be compared to recovering from a serious illness. It will require many adjustments and may take several years.

One of the adjustments the Witness will need to address is his fear of being outside of the "ark of the Watchtower organization." *That safety net was all he knew.*

He will have to reorient his view of life in general, because his outlook was through the lenses of the Watchtower and he was accustomed to being dependent on it as his source of stability and his safety net. Now it's gone.

But it was necessary if he is to have an unclouded view and a relationship with the real Jesus — the Jesus of the Bible — not the Jesus of The Watchtower.

Now you have a basic understanding of what the Witness will face if he leaves his religion.

The Loss of Family and Security

Once your Witness friend leaves the Watchtower organization, you need to know that he will be completely cast out and rejected by those he loves:

- Family
- Friends
- His Kingdom Hall associates
- Co-workers

In short, his relationships will cease with all Witnesses — even if it's a wife, husband, children, brother, sister, aunt, uncle — it doesn't matter. *He will be disfellowshipped (excommunicated), considered as dead and will be shunned by those he loves.*

As he contemplates leaving, he knows what it will cost him and it will weigh heavily upon his heart. Because he is a Witness, his only associations have been with other Witnesses.

The disfellowshipping (or excommunication) of one of Jehovah's Witnesses is both harsh and brutal. It is the severest penalty they suffer and the most feared. He no longer exists as a person and is considered both a traitor and apostate. His own children will address him as such and turn their backs.

The first few weeks (or months) after his disfellowshipping will be the most critical. **By being rejected he will be alone.** The severity of the trauma of disfellowshipping will also depend on how long he was in the organization.

To be disfellowshipped is not only to suffer rejection by family and friends but by "Jehovah God Himself" and "His" organization — the Watchtower Society — "the ark of salvation." It is the most humiliating and degrading experience a Witness can face; and it is done at the Kingdom Hall, whether he is there for it or not. *Everyone* will know.

The adjustment into his new life may take many years. The lifestyle he enjoyed as one of Jehovah's Witnesses is now threatened. Many may not leave the Watchtower because the cost is too great. And if they do leave, tremendous guilt sets in because they are no longer doing what was required of them to "please Jehovah and his organization." That was the life he was accustomed to and was all he knew.

Once he leaves, however, he will need a recovery time, like one who was severely ill. During this time he will experience a wide range of emotions:

- Fear
- Anger
- Depression
- Disappointment
- Frustration
- Anxiety
- Failure
- Defeat

He may also be left with the pain and sorrow of all those wasted years, believing that Armageddon was always near. Because of this imminent danger of Armageddon, many couples never had children, college degrees were never earned and the desire for a fulfilling career was never achieved.

He may also have feelings of being used. After all, the religion required him to attend meetings five days a week and spend all his time reading nothing but *Watchtower* literature. The substance of his life was woven into the fabric of the Watchtower Society.[1]

---

1) For more information, see *Jehovah's Witnesses and the Problem of Mental Illness* by Dr. Jerry Bergman, Ph.D. (1992).

Holding on to What Was

I remember a former Jehovah's Witness who attended a church where I was on staff. She was a faithful member of the church and was on fire for Jesus. She had written a letter to her Kingdom Hall and disassociated herself from the Watchtower organization a few years before.

Although she was born again, she still would not accept a blood transfusion and could not celebrate Christmas with a clean conscience. She was scarred by her former beliefs. Although she knew Jesus as her Saviour and Lord, her past life still haunted her.

While attending an ex-Jehovah's Witness convention, I spoke with another woman who had left the Watchtower organization two years before. She was born into a Witness family and left the organization when she was 25. As she looked at *the Watchtower* literature I had, with tears streaming down her face, she said:

> "I loved Jehovah. I gave 25-years of my life to
> The Watchtower and loved Jehovah."

After a brief conversation, she admitted that the Jehovah whom she fell in love with was a cruel hoax —the false god portrayed in the *Watchtower's* publications.

Many Witnesses who have left the Watchtower are like those who return from war and have a difficult time reorienting themselves back into society.

They are also like those who have been institutionalized

most of their life and cannot adjust to society. Some deliberately sabotage their freedom by breaking the law and return to prison.

Such is the challenge for those who gave themselves to the Watchtower Bible and Tract Society as one of Jehovah's Witnesses.

This is a religion that prides itself in being different from the rest of society. Members of this sect pride themselves in their religion, "taking a stand for their faith" by refusing:

- To salute the flag of their country
- To stand for the national anthem
- To celebrate birthdays, Christmas, Easter, Mother's Day, Father's Day, etc.
- Blood transfusions

Upon leaving this religion, the Witness knows that he will lose the "status" of being different by falling to the ranks of the status quo. That sense of pride is woven into his self-esteem giving him a sense of worth, because *he was not like everyone else. This was his identity.*

Once you have successfully led the Witness out of the Watchtower Society, be sensitive to what he is feeling.

Disciple with Patience

When I was a little boy our family took a trip to Disneyland. Out of curiosity I left the protection of my parents and went wandering around. I was fascinated by the sights and sounds of this great theme park; but I was also lost.

With tears streaming down my face, I asked everyone I bumped into if they had seen my parents. Of course, it never occurred to me that no one knew who my family was. I was just scared and panicked.

Just then, a uniformed officer noticed me and asked me if I was lost. Together, we went looking for my mom and dad. Eventually, my family and I were reunited. Even though I was in tears, I felt tremendous peace as I embraced my parents.

These emotions are much like the feelings of Witnesses who leave the Watchtower — at first a sense of deep loss and estrangement. They need a home, a place where they can feel secure, loved and accepted. Just like I felt that sense of security when I was reunited with my family, the Witnesses feel that same sense of security within the Watchtower Society.

When they leave that place of security (like I did that day) and realize what they have lost, the only thing in their mind is to find a security zone —and fast!

Even as that police officer was patient and caring, and was intent on reuniting me with my family, you have the opportunity to direct the Witness to a life of security, by being his friend, reorienting him back into society and discipling him in his walk with Christ. Because there may be pockets of *Watchtower* theology imbedded in his thinking, you will need to exercise patience during the discipling process.

Let me remind you: you will need to patiently go over

with him those witnessing strategies that challenged and compromised his belief structure. This will further cement in his mind that The Watchtower Society cannot be trusted ever again. You will also need to ask him if he can fully trust the Watchtower Society again.

Remember, the Witness has given years to The Watchtower Society. All he knows is *Watchtower* theology and he may still reject some true Christian beliefs. Only the Holy Spirit can convince him of the error of his former belief system.

CHAPTER 7

Showing the Plan of Salvation

Perhaps you have met one of Jehovah's Witnesses at your doorstep or you may even have family members or friends in the Watchtower Society — and your witnessing fell on deaf ears. Be encouraged: you now have a plan and successful field-proven strategies to win that Witness to Christ.

And what is your plan?

1. Avoid the "flash point" of arguments: the Bible. *Never* discuss or argue theology or scripture.

2. Your strategy is to weaken and destroy the supply line that feeds the Witnesses: the Watchtower publications.

3. This is done by **asking the Witnesses if their publications are inspired**. Your advantage is that the Watchtower *admits* their publications are **not** inspired, and that they have made prophetic mistakes. This shows that their leadership never heard from God in the first place.

4. Add seeds of doubt in their minds until their confidence in the Watchtower Society has been destroyed. You can do this by showing specific places in *The Watchtower* where 1) it contradicts itself and 2) it clearly contradicts the Bible.

5. Once the Jehovah's Witness's confidence in his organization has been destroyed, he can no longer appeal to what he had been taught from the Watchtower's publications. You will then have a candidate ready to listen to the gospel.

I urge you to write down these principles so you can follow an outline in your presentation. Because the Witnesses are accustomed to following the Society's style of teaching, your presentation will be done in the same manner as a *Watchtower* study — without *The Watchtower*, of course.

• If he brings up any theological objections during the course of this study, remind him that his objections are based only on *The Watchtower's* uninspired teachings, written by uninspired men who never really heard from God.

His whole belief system must be restructured with Biblical principles free from Watchtower influence.

You will need to continue planting seeds of doubt in his mind. Remind him that there is no good purpose or eternal value in the uninspired *Watchtower* and the "God" he once believed in. Use this doubt to your advantage in your journey towards leading him to Christ. The doubt will soon be replaced by faith.

Your Witnessing Strategy

No General would ever lead his soldiers into a conflict without a strategic plan. In order to achieve victory, the soldier will always train before his deployment for battle in the strategy his leadership has planned. By following the bulleted points below, you can achieve victory by rescuing a lost Jehovah's Witness.

• Get the Witness to understand that, though they claim to use the Bible, they *really* use *The Watchtower* as their primary books for study. (See Chapter 2 for questions that will help you get started.)

• **Do not quote scriptures to make your points.** Use simple logic, comparing the Bible to the uninspired *Watchtower*. Your strategy is to get the Witnesses to think: which has greater purpose and eternal value, the Bible or the uninspired *Watchtower*? The Witness's position will begin to weaken.

• If you need to give him further evidence to prove your case that the Society is not inspired, show him how The Watchtower made a huge mistake by saying Jesus died on a "torture stake," and not a cross. (See Chapter 4.)

• Point out the fact that *The Watchtower* has three inconsistent views as to the identity of the One Who resurrected Jesus. (See Chapter 5.)

Pray. Then don't worry. God will guide you.

As you gain practice, you will eventually understand their tactics and recognize their weaknesses.

Regardless what he uses to defend what he was taught, *remind him that everything he believes was founded upon uninspired writings.* **This is a key point.**

Jehovah's Witness Tactics

The Witnesses are thoroughly trained to be in complete control. Listen attentively to how they try to control the conversation. **Never** allow that to happen.

Once the Witnesses are caught out in the open and are vulnerable, they will change the subject and gear the conversation to another area with clever subtlety. If that happens, ask questions such as, "Aren't you interested in what we were talking about?" Or, "This area is important to me, why isn't it important to you?" "Is my question forcing you to avoid the truth of this whole matter?"

As I presented my case to a veteran Jehovah's Witness, I noted she was restless. Out of nowhere she asked me if I celebrated Christmas. She changed the subject for two reasons:

1. To avoid the issue by getting me to defend what she believed I was doing during the Holiday season.

2. To avoid the issue I was talking about by changing the subject. This way, she could regain control of the conversation by steering me in another direction — onto her playing field.

Point: Stick to the issue in your discussion. Do not allow yourself to be sidetracked.

Although the Witnesses use the Bible as part of their message, **do not fall for the trap of arguing scripture**. The *New World Translation* is a biased translation, specifically written for the Witnesses to cement *Watchtower* theology. Once you fall into their trap of arguing scripture you will lose your witness and will be on *their* territory. He will argue what he believes to be true from his own Bible. You will be on the defensive and will have no impact in your witnessing. You *will* be frustrated.

Questions for the Witness

Keep in mind that the Witnesses do not understand salvation in the sense that you do. In his mind, salvation is only reserved for a select few of 144,000. *After* **he has rejected the authority of the Watchtower Society, you will finally get to use your Bible and actually witness to the former Witness and introduce him to Christ.**

A word of caution: do not use any scripture and then give your own personal interpretation, or he may take a defensive posture. *Allow the scriptures to interpret themselves.* Remember, he believed that you were a pagan. He may still be wrestling with that issue and may not fully trust you.

You are going to ask a series of questions and *point to the scripture* **which will be his answer**. This is the way he was trained to study the Bible through *The Watchtower*. You are going to use *this same method* to lead him to Christ. He may not trust you, but he will trust the Bible.

Once you start the actual process of leading him to Christ, until he decides to trust you and your King James Bible, you will need to use his *New World Translation*.

Because the Watchtower Society has already published King James Bibles, he will be able to transition from the *New World Translation* to the King James Version. Remind the Witness that the Watchtower Society used King James Bibles until 1949. Certainly, it must be a trustworthy Bible if they are still producing it today.

The following are questions you can ask.

• **Why is it important to be born again?**

> Unless **anyone** is born again, he cannot see the kingdom of God.[1]

• **Who can be born again?**

> **Everyone** believing that Jesus is the Christ has been born from God...[2]

We must place our trust in Jesus Christ to be born again.

• **Was there urgency in Jesus' words when he said you must be born again?**

---

1) John 3:3, *New World Translation*, 1984 edition (emphasis added).
2) I John 5:1, *New World Translation*, 1984 edition (emphasis added).

Do not marvel because I told you, **YOU** people **must** be born again.[3]

• **What is the reward of those who are born again?**

"Jesus answered: Most truly I say to you, Unless **anyone** is born from water and spirit, he cannot **enter into the kingdom of God**.[4]

You can also ask questions like:

• Did you notice that Jesus repeated important words like "anyone," "everyone," "YOU people" in these scriptures?

• When you read these scriptures, who does "anyone," "everyone," and "YOU people"include?

• Does it leave anyone out?

• Would you agree that those words *include* you?

• Did you know that in 1886, the Watchtower said:

"...the only ground of salvation mentioned in the scriptures is faith in Christ as our Redeemer and Lord. "By grace are ye saved through faith. Eph. 2:8."[5]

"The only way, by which any and all of the condemned race may come to God, is not by meritorious works, neither by ignorance, but by faith in the precious blood of Christ,

---

3) John 3:7, *New World Translation*, 1984 edition (emphasis added).
4) John 3:5, *New World Translation*, 1984 edition (emphasis added).
5) *The Divine Plan of the Ages* (1886), p. 100.

which taketh away the sin of the world.
(I Peter 1:19; John 1:29.) This is the gospel,
the good tidings of great joy, which shall be
unto ALL PEOPLE."[6]

- What is the only ground of salvation mentioned
  in the scriptures?

- What is the only way any and all of the
  condemned race may come to God?

Remember: The Witness has been taught that he will remain on *Paradise Earth* as part of a *Great Crowd*. While that may be in the forefront of his mind, remind him that he has seen that *The Watchtower* was never inspired and that the **only truth that matters now is what the Bible says.**

He may need to re-read the scriptures stated earlier to plant seeds of faith in his heart. You will be amazed how fast faith will change the focus of his heart once he starts to doubt *The Watchtower.*

- **Ask him to read John 6:35-40**

  - Who is the Bread of Life?

  - How will Jesus respond to those who come to Him?[7]
  - What is promised to those who believe on the Son?[8]
  - Jesus made another promise to those who believe
    on Him. What is it?[9]

---

6) *The Divine Plan,* p. 103.
7) John 6:37.
8) John 6:40.
9) John 6:47.

You may ask:

- Remember what you read about "anyone,"
  "everyone" and "YOU?" Is the Bible personally
  including you?
- What is the Bible teaching in John 6:35-40, 47?

Ask him to read John 3:15, 16

- What word is used for those who believe in Jesus?
  Does that include you, too?
  Answer: Yes

Ask him to read John 14:6

> Jesus said unto him: 'I am the way and the
> truth and the life. No one comes to the Fa-
> ther except through me.'[10]

- What was Jesus' claim in this passage?
- If Jesus' claim is true, is there any other
  way to the Father?

Ask him to read Acts 4:10-12

- What name under heaven is given among
  men whereby we must be saved?

Ask him to read Acts 8:26-39

- After Philip witnessed to an Ethiopian, the
  Ethiopian asked if he could now be baptized.
  Philip replied:

  …'If thou believest with all thine heart, thou

---

10) *The New World Translation*, 1984 edition.

> mayest.' And he answered and said, 'I believe
> that Jesus Christ is the Son of God.'[11]

The former Witness will have to read this passage from your King James Bible and you will need to point out that Acts 8:37 is *missing* from the *New World Translation*. I believe it was deleted by The Watchtower's translation committee to keep this crucial truth away from the Witnesses.

Note: The Witness should be able to locate a King James Bible at the Kingdom Hall's Theocratic library. Or he can order one through the Watchtower Society's Headquarters in Brooklyn, New York.

You may also state that the Watchtower Society would surely never print an unreliable Bible for their followers.

Ask: Because the Ethiopian made this confession of faith, does this mean that he was saved before he was baptized?

Ask him to read Acts 9:20

- Why did Saul preach that Christ is the Son of God?
- What was the purpose of this message?
- How does this tie into the Ethiopian's confession of faith?

Ask Him To Read Romans 3: 22-24

> "Yes, God's righteousness through the faith
> in Jesus Christ, for all those having faith. For
> there is no distinction. For all have sinned
> and fall short of the glory of God, and it is as

---

11) Acts 8:37 (KJV).

a free gift that they are being declared righteous by his underserved kindness through the release by the ransom [paid] by Jesus Christ."[12]

- What is available for all who have faith?
- What free gift is this passage referring to?
- Does this free gift pertain to all?

Ask Him To Read Romans 6:23

- By what gift is everlasting life?

Ask: How is one saved? Then have him read Romans 10:9-10. What is the formula for salvation?

Answer: Confessing with the mouth the Lord Jesus and believing with the heart that God has raised Him from the dead.

Have him read Ephesians 2:8-9

• Is salvation through faith or is it something you have to work for?

You might say: I know that you worked in the organization to gain God's favor and avoid destruction at Armageddon, but what kind of works does God require from you?

• Have him read John 6: 28-29

Therefore they said to him: 'What shall we do to work the works of God?' In answer, Jesus said to them: "This is the work of God,

---

12) *New World Translation*, 1984 edition (emphasis added).

that YOU exercise faith in him whom that ONE sent forth.'[13]

You are now ready to introduce the former Witness to the Son of God. Everything you have studied, prayed for and applied from the principles in this book has come down to this one moment: *salvation* for the former Jehovah's Witness. This is the purpose of all your note taking, rehearsing and time you have spent with the Witness.

At this point, there are numerous scriptures you can use to invite the Jehovah's Witness to receive Jesus. Here are a few suggestions:

> For whosoever shall call upon the name of the Lord shall be saved. (Romans 10:13)

> Verily, verily, I say unto you, He that believeth on me hath everlasting life. (John 6:47)

> For by grace are ye saved through faith; and that not of yourselves: it is the gift of God: Not of works, lest any man should boast. (Ephesians 2:8-9).

Here is a suggested way to use a Bible verse:

> Behold, I stand at the door, and knock: if any man hear my voice, and open the door, I will come in to him, and will sup with him, and he with me. (Revelation 3:20)

Christian: Jesus is standing at the door and knocking. **He**

---

13) *New World Translation*, 1984 edition.

wants to come in to your heart! He also said that if *any-one* hears His voice and opens the door, He will come into your house and take the evening meal with you and you with Him. You can be saved and have fellowship with the Saviour. This is His desire for you.

Christian: If you do not wish to leave Him standing at the door, then *let Him in*. When He comes into your life you will have the gift of eternal life, as well as fellowship with Him, and He with you.

Christian: I know that you may feel uneasy or even apprehensive in praying on your own so allow me to give you some guidelines as to what to pray:

> "Father, I thought I was serving You through the Watchtower Society. I was wrong. I ask You to not only forgive me from serving in a false organization but forgive my sins. I repent and turn away from the authority of the Watchtower Society and from my sins. According to Your Word, I confess that Jesus is the Lord and only Saviour and I believe in my heart that God has raised Him from the dead. I now realize there is nothing I could ever do to gain Your favor except to believe on the Lord Jesus Christ. I ask You to come into my heart and to be my Saviour. Thank You for Your mercy, Your grace and Your love for me. I now accept You as my Lord and Saviour and will serve You and You only the rest

of my days. These things I declare by faith
and declare my faith in Jesus, the Son of God.
In Jesus' Name, Amen."

Congratulations! You have now rescued one of Jehovah's
Witnesses from the power and authority of *The Watchtower*
into the Kingdom of God.

Now your work discipling this new Christian begins. I
encourage you to take to heart the guidelines in Chapter 8
that deal with issues he may face during this time.

This is also a time when you can use the scriptures to
encourage his heart as he begins this new walk with Christ;
but you must always be in prayer for your new brother or
sister in Christ. During this transition, his life will have to
start all over. But you will be there to love, nurture and edify
your new brother or sister.

Not only does your ex-Witness friend have a testimony,
you do too. You can finally testify to others that with the
Lord's wisdom and proven witnessing techniques, *anyone*
can lead one of Jehovah's Witnesses out of the *Watchtower*
and into the saving grace of our Lord and Saviour Jesus
Christ.

CHAPTER 8

The Journey into Grace

Once the Witness rejects the authority of The Watchtower Society, his *Journey into Grace* begins. As one of Jehovah's Witnesses, he could only hope that if he worked hard enough for his religion he might "make it" and avoid destruction at Armageddon. His "salvation" was based on works, the things he was mandated to do by the Watchtower Society —or else.

Now that he can read the Bible without *The Watchtower's* color-coated lenses, here is your chance to minister to him the Word of God, unfiltered by *The Watchtower's* interpretations. However, as you disciple the ex-Witness, you will have to help him discern and separate Watchtower theology from *his* understanding of the scriptures.

Discipling Tips

• Stay away from subjects such as the celebration of holidays, birthdays, military service, politics and blood transfusions — issues he found offensive while he was in The Watchtower Society. He will eventually work them out.

• Also stay away from scriptures pertaining to life after death, hell, the trinity, the 144,000 (Revelation 7) and the soul. He was thoroughly trained how to debate these issues. Do not debate him on these issues.

These issues will be addressed eventually, but until then you will work on other areas of his spiritual life. This will require your patience and understanding during his transition out of the mindset of The Watchtower Society, as he integrates into society and learns about true Christianity.

Share Your Testimony

His *Journey into Grace* will begin with you and your testimony. Tell him who you once were and how you came to know Jesus as your Saviour and Lord.

Tell him about the peace and assurance you have, not because you go to a Christian church, but because Jesus has transformed your life. Let him know how your relationship with Christ has changed your marriage, your relationships with your children, grandchildren, extended family, friends, business associates and others (however it applies to you).

Assure the ex-Witness that the change you have experienced in your heart can shortly be his testimony also. **He may need to be re-assured again and again**.

Engage in Activities

There are some activities you can do together during his *Journey into Grace* that will help him transition out of The Watchtower Society. While these activities may appear to have no value, be assured they have a definite purpose:

1. **Talk with him.** More importantly, listen to him. He will have much to say as he expresses his feelings.

2. **Assure him** that the emotions he is experiencing after leaving The Watchtower Society are normal. Assure him that, as he embarks on a new life in Christ, there will be a *freshness* to his existence and purpose in life; those negative emotions will eventually go away.

3. **Look** for symptoms of depression. If any arise, **encourage** him to keep busy. He may need to begin outdoor activities such as hiking, walking, jogging, swimming and/or bike riding. Indoor activities can include re-organizing his home, his garage, painting, landscaping or finding a hobby. *He needs to keep busy.*

4. **Help him replace what was lost: friends.** Introduce him to friends you trust who will listen to him and encourage him. Pick friends who will enjoy activities with him like those listed in #3.

5. When he reads the Bible, ask if you can **join him** and

read it together. If he asks questions and you don't have an answer, be honest by saying, "I don't know but I *will* find out." Be true to your word and get the answer for him.

By being his friend and doing these things you are not only helping him transition out of The Watchtower, you are also helping him discover a new life in Christ. You are being a testimony to him by showing him that you really do care for him and that the Christian life is filled with peace and joy.

As time goes by, he will have a sense of belonging by becoming a part of the family of God, and not part of a religion. He is already suspicious of religion. He needs to begin understanding his new relationship with Jesus Christ.

The Issue of Trust

Earlier, I told about the Witness who cried, "If Jehovah failed me, what guarantee can you give me that Jesus won't fail me too?" After he and his wife accepted Christ, his wife admitted there was an issue of trusting God, ever since they learned that The Watchtower Society had deceived them about who Jehovah God was.

That's why it is crucial that you *keep your promises!* Remember, The Watchtower Society also made promises by declaring who God was, and it turned out to be false.

He needs to learn to trust all over again. And that trust will start with **you**. After all, he once believed you were a pagan, remember?

Once he learns to trust you he will see Christ in you and eventually learn to trust Christ Himself. This is why sharing your testimony of how Christ changed your heart and life is so important. He once knew the letter of the law — The Watchtower — not the life-changing experience of accepting the finished work of the Lord Jesus Christ that you have experienced. This also is part of his *Journey into Grace.*

The Decision for Christ

Following are some pointers to help you disciple the ex-Witness. You may need to write down key things you wish to share with the ex-Witness.

Understand this: Even after he has left The Watchtower Society, **he will still have the desire to work for the Kingdom to gain God's favor.** This will be one of the last footholds of The Watchtower's influence to be removed: works. Jesus addressed the issue of working the works of God:

> Then said they unto him, *What shall we do, that we might work the works of God?* Jesus answered and said unto them, *This is the work of God, that ye believe on him whom he hath sent.*[1]

This statement may be foreign to the ex-Witness. The only works he is familiar with are attending all The Watchtower-sponsored meetings and door-to-door activities. But there is **only one way** to work the works of God: **believe on the Lord Jesus Christ.**

1) John 6:29. Emphasis added.

In Paul's letter to the Ephesians, he wrote:

> For *by grace are ye saved* through faith; and
> that not of yourselves: *it is the gift of God:* Not
> of works, lest any man should boast.[2]

Ephesians 2:8-9 is the perfect scripture for the ex-Witness because it speaks of God's grace. The word "grace" in this text deals specifically with removing guilt. God's grace removes guilt.

The ex-Witness may feel guilt on several fronts:

• Abandoning the faith he once believed to be true.

• Not working to please Jehovah.

• The sense of wasted years in The Watchtower Society.

• The sense of guilt for those he proselytized into the Watchtower organization.

• Being disfellowshipped and being cut off from family and friends.

God's forgiveness is not just an act of mercy or compassion. His grace to forgive us removes the misery of guilt and the condemnation we feel because of what we've done or because of a broken life.

God knows the power of guilt and the condemnation it brings; but because of His great love, we are saved by His grace —that power that removes guilt. That condemnation has now been confronted by God, Who Himself is Grace.

---

2) Ephesians 2:8-9. Emphasis added.

God Loves to Give

When I was in Junior High, I entered a school-wide competition of selling household cleaning products to raise money for my school. The contestant who sold the most products would win a stereo. That stereo was everything a teenager would want; and I was determined to make it mine.

Day after day and week after week, I went door-to-door selling as much as I could. I poured my whole heart into making every sales pitch count. With every sale I was that much closer to being called on stage and given that stereo.

The day finally came for the winner to be announced. I had sold over 180 cases. That translated to 720 one-gallon bottles. I was sure to win.

I lost.

I was crushed. I had worked so hard because I had my heart set on winning that stereo. That evening, as my Dad and I were driving home from church, I told him how I was so disappointed. Little did I know that I was about to experience a miracle.

A family member had heard that I had lost. She had bought a brand-new Sanyo stereo for herself. But out of love she went to our house and hooked it up in my room. When we got home, I went to my room and turned on the light. There on my dresser was a brand new stereo, plugged in and ready to go.

When I saw it I took a deep breath and just stood at the doorway. I wept. Someone blessed me with a gift. I did not earn it; it was given to me out of love. That other stereo represented all my labor but it was ultimately lost. The stereo before me represented someone else's love for me.

The gift that was given to me on that wonderful day removed the misery of my loss earlier that day. The gift was not the stereo, it was my aunt's **grace** for me.

This is but a miniscule example of God's greater love for us: His grace. God loves to give. And in His grace — that power to remove guilt — we are saved through faith by simply believing.

There is a repetitive pattern in these next scriptures with respect to God's grace. The purpose of a pattern is to reveal what its creator intends for us to see: Here, God's gift.

Ephesians 2:8 declares that his grace provides His gift: eternal life.

Romans 6:23 declares:

> … *the gift of God* is eternal life through Jesus Christ our Lord.

John 3:16 states:

> For God so loved the world, that *he gave* his only begotten Son, that whosoever believeth in him should not perish, but have everlasting life.[3]

---

3) Emphasis added.

These are examples of God deliberately repeating Himself to get us to believe that **we do not have to work to merit His favor.** Through His favor we receive His gift. The stereo given to me on was not the result of my work. It was a result of someone's grace because of her love for me. I didn't earn it; grace gave it to me out of love.

The *Journey to Grace* for those who exit the Watchtower organization will subject them to tremendous loss, pain and grief. But in that pain stands the grace of God, ready to touch that broken life with the embracing arms of our Lord and Saviour, Jesus Christ.

May God bless you as you give an answer to those precious Jehovah's Witnesses you encounter in your walk with Christ. Amen.

Notes:

<u>Notes</u>:

<u>Notes</u>:

<u>Notes</u>:

<u>Notes</u>: